W9-AJN-258

CREEPY CRAWLIES

Praying Mantises

by Megan Borgert-Spaniol

BLASTOFF! READERS

BELLWETHER MEDIA • MINNEAPOLIS, MN

Note to Librarians, Teachers, and Parents:

Blastoff! Readers are carefully developed by literacy experts and combine standards-based content with developmentally appropriate text.

Level 1 provides the most support through repetition of high-frequency words, light text, predictable sentence patterns, and strong visual support.

Level 2 offers early readers a bit more challenge through varied simple sentences, increased text load, and less repetition of high-frequency words.

Level 3 advances early-fluent readers toward fluency through increased text and concept load, less reliance on visuals, longer sentences, and more literary language.

Level 4 builds reading stamina by providing more text per page, increased use of punctuation, greater variation in sentence patterns, and increasingly challenging vocabulary.

Level 5 encourages children to move from "learning to read" to "reading to learn" by providing even more text, varied writing styles, and less familiar topics.

Whichever book is right for your reader, Blastoff! Readers are the perfect books to build confidence and encourage a love of reading that will last a lifetime!

This edition first published in 2016 by Bellwether Media, Inc.

No part of this publication may be reproduced in whole or in part without written permission of the publisher. For information regarding permission, write to Bellwether Media, Inc., Attention: Permissions Department, 5357 Penn Avenue South, Minneapolis, MN 55419.

Library of Congress Cataloging-in-Publication Data

Borgert-Spaniol, Megan, 1989-
  Praying Mantises / by Megan Borgert-Spaniol.
    pages cm. – (Blastoff! readers. Creepy Crawlies)
  Summary: "Developed by literacy experts for students in kindergarten through grade three, this book introduces praying mantises to young readers through leveled text and related photos"– Provided by publisher.
  Audience: Ages 5-8.
  Audience: K to grade 3.
  Includes bibliographical references and index.
  ISBN 978-1-62617-300-2 (hardcover : alk. paper)
  1. Praying mantis–Juvenile literature. I. Title.
  QL505.9.M35B67 2016
  595.7'27–dc23
                    2015028687

Printed in the United States of America, North Mankato, MN.

Table of Contents

Hidden Hunters

Praying mantises are sneaky **insects**. Their bodies blend in with trees, grass, and rocks.

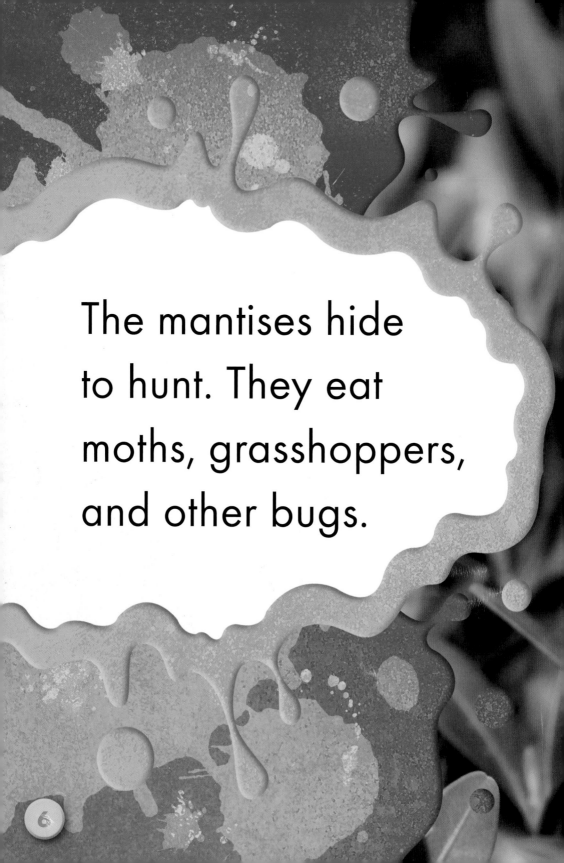

The mantises hide
to hunt. They eat
moths, grasshoppers,
and other bugs.

Their heads turn from side to side to look for food.

Flash Attack

Praying mantises stay still until **prey** is near. Then they attack in a flash!

Spines on their front legs trap the prey.

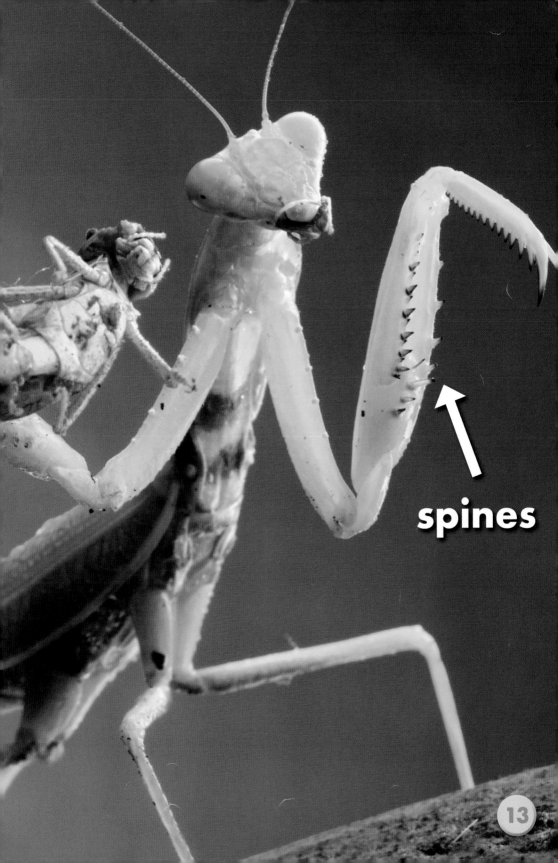

spines

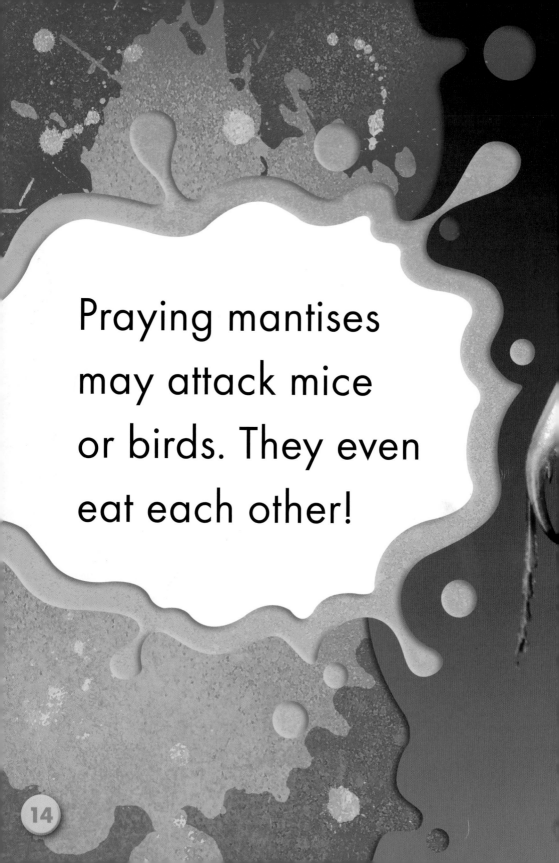

Praying mantises may attack mice or birds. They even eat each other!

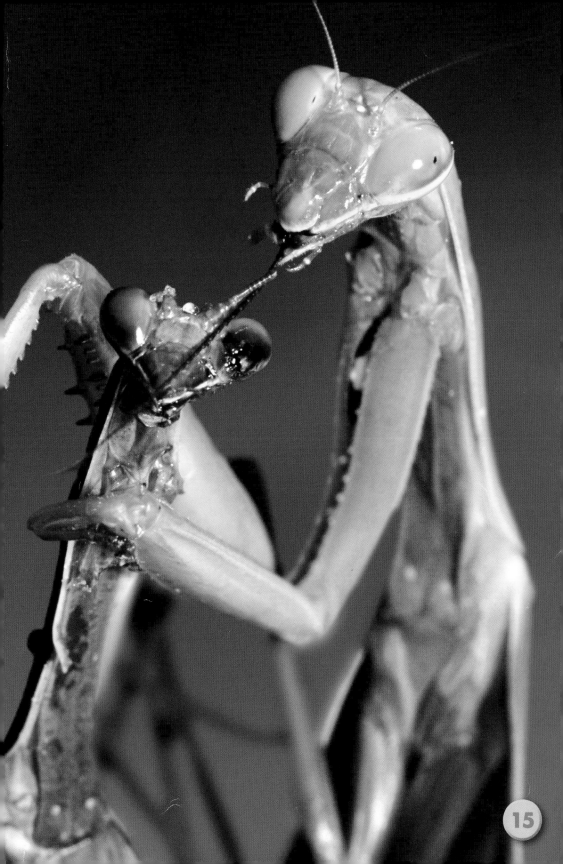

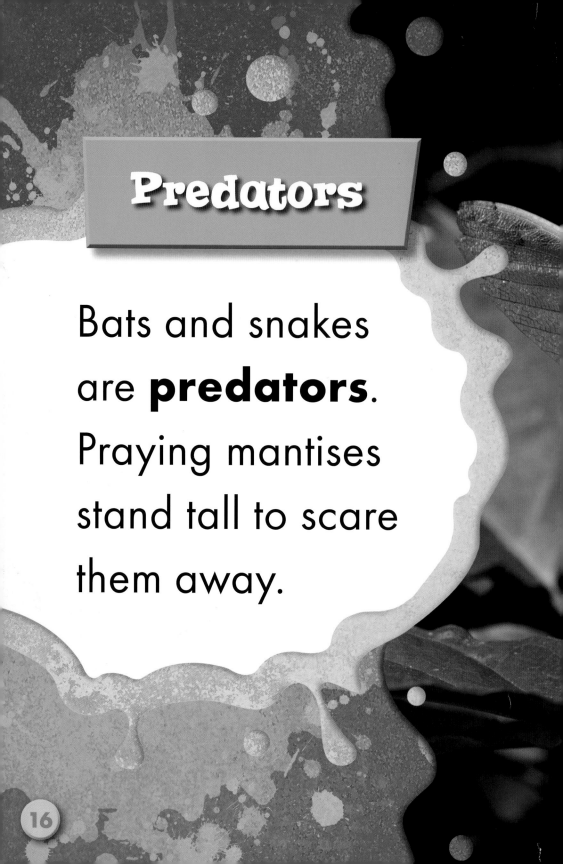

Predators

Bats and snakes are **predators**. Praying mantises stand tall to scare them away.

Nymphs

Female praying mantises lay their eggs on twigs. Babies **hatch** in spring.

19

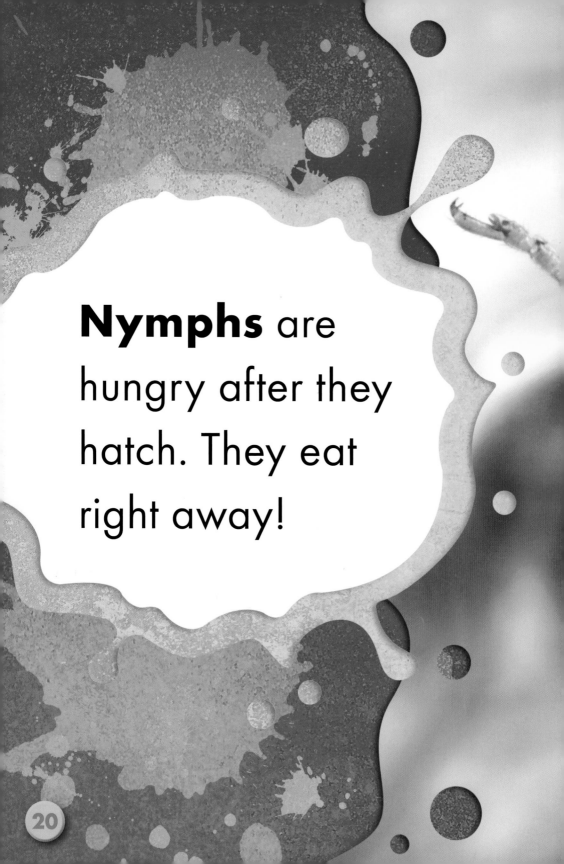

Nymphs are hungry after they hatch. They eat right away!

Glossary

hatch—to break out of an egg

insects—small animals with six legs and hard outer bodies; an insect's body is divided into three parts.

nymphs—baby praying mantises

predators—animals that hunt other animals for food

prey—animals that are hunted by other animals for food

spines—hard spikes on the front legs of praying mantises; spines help the insects hold on to prey.

To Learn More

AT THE LIBRARY

Bodden, Valerie. *Mantises*. Mankato, Minn.: Creative Paperbacks, 2011.

Goldish, Meish. *Deadly Praying Mantises*. New York, N.Y.: Bearport Pub. Co., 2008.

Roza, Greg. *Mysterious Mantises*. New York, N.Y.: Gareth Stevens Pub., 2011.

ON THE WEB

Learning more about praying mantises is as easy as 1, 2, 3.

1. Go to www.factsurfer.com.

2. Enter "praying mantises" into the search box.

3. Click the "Surf" button and you will see a list of related web sites.

With factsurfer.com, finding more information is just a click away.

Index

The images in this book are reproduced through the courtesy of: Igor Siwanowicz, front cover; Czesznak Zsolt, pp. 4-5; Rob Byron, pp. 6-7; Andrii Muzyka, pp. 8-9; Cathy Keifer, pp. 10-11, 18-19; Kristina Postnikova, pp. 12-13; Francesco Tomasinelli/ Science Source, pp. 14-15; Mitsuhiko Imamori/ Corbis, pp. 16-17; Alex Wild/ Corbis, pp. 20-21.